Happy New Year, Aunt Maxine and Uncle Bob.
I love you.
Sue

"This writing should be read by everyone."

Charles L. Royce, President
Royce Rolls Ringer Company
Grand Rapids, Michigan, USA

THE TRAVELER ~ GLOWING POWER

SUE DEAN

Painted Wheel Box 81406 Albuquerque, NM 87108

Printed on 100% acid-free, recycled paper.

ISBN: 1-884385-15-X

Contents

Lulled by the rails, the traveler gazed out her train window at scenes flickering in the chill winter sunshine. Faraway memories languidly mingled with daydreams of destinations unknown. Relaxed and warm, she looked forward to the journey ahead.

A touch on the arm roused her. It was a small child looking into her eyes, expecting to be lifted onto her lap. She reached for him.

Other people drew toward them and settled around. The traveler had not met them before, and many were strangers to each other, yet there was a feeling of camaraderie and ease. They were waiting for her to speak . . .

As this child was born, so in birth are we brought upon the earth.

But not in birth are we sustained.

Some of us were fortunate to be born to soul-mentors,

parents who delighted in us and understood us.

They nourished the dreams of our hearts

as they nourished our bodies.

They could not fill every need we had, for no one can,

but they gave us a heritage of confidence and trust,

to cushion us always.

Some of us were not quite so fortunate. We were born to parents who could not be soul-mentors to us for a singular reason —

wounds from their pasts had not yet been healed.

From them we received conflicting messages.

They spoke kind words of appreciation, then unexplainably

harsh words to tame our child spirit.

Their inheritance to us was anxiety.

We grew up not truly in touch with them, or with ourselves.

They taught us and gave us as much as they could . . .

But how were they to know what we needed when they were

unaware of their own needs?

The rail cars sped by small towns and rural scenes. Fields and fences spread themselves across the land like a garden-green patchwork quilt . . .

To each of you who feel yourself to be a soul-orphan I say

It is time to waken yourself to your own special identity.

Do not hide the truth from yourself. Examine what has happened,

learn from it, feel it, then let it float away from your memory,

forever.

Surround yourself with loving people who respect you and listen to you with sensitivity, people who cherish you.

You have a right to be yourself — totally, honestly, joyfully yourself.

You have a right

to express

yourself.

You are important.

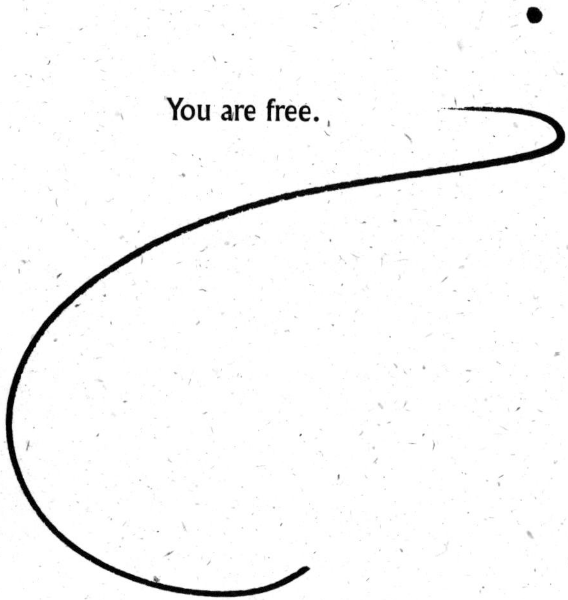

You are free.

As the train streaked through the heavy velvet of night, the traveler and her companions pressed their faces to the cold windows to view a sudden storm. Lightning zagged across the dark sky, knifing in dazzling white bolts from cloud to earth. Thunder rolled in reply. It proclaimed its power to mortals below.

People conversed in bits of words and silences. Gradually, they began asking the traveler questions about their own power . . .

We each have more power than a lightning bolt. It pulses inside us every moment of every day that we are alive. It is vital. It is real.

It produces intense surges of energy. But it can be repressed. Then, instead of being a benefit to us, it is a curse.

When we imprison our inner power by not using it, it betrays us.

It renders us impotent when we need strength,
heavy-handed when we need tenderness,
dull-witted when we need perception,
wakeful when we need sleep.

The force

of our power

when denied

and unused

puts us

out of touch

with ourselves.

Lightning flashed. Thunder rumbled like deep heathen kettle drums as it played out its reverberating concert in the sky. Tremors shimmied across the land toward the moving train . . .

Inner power lights your entire being, as if a glowing segment of lightning rested inside you.

Treat it gently, humbly. Just as it can be unused, so can it be falsely used. It can be exploited for status or prestige, rather than dedicated to the expression of your soul.

Listen to the still quiet Voice within you.

Then you know with certainty how to use and direct your power.

Rejoice that you have this awesome force within you.

Open yourself to its deepest expression and

transform your life.

∞

Morning brought brightness and warmth — and arrival at their destination. Children from the train went with the traveler, down the hill, into the town. They talked as they tramped and laughed as they leapt.

This is what they all sang . . .

Energy flows from our heads to our toes.

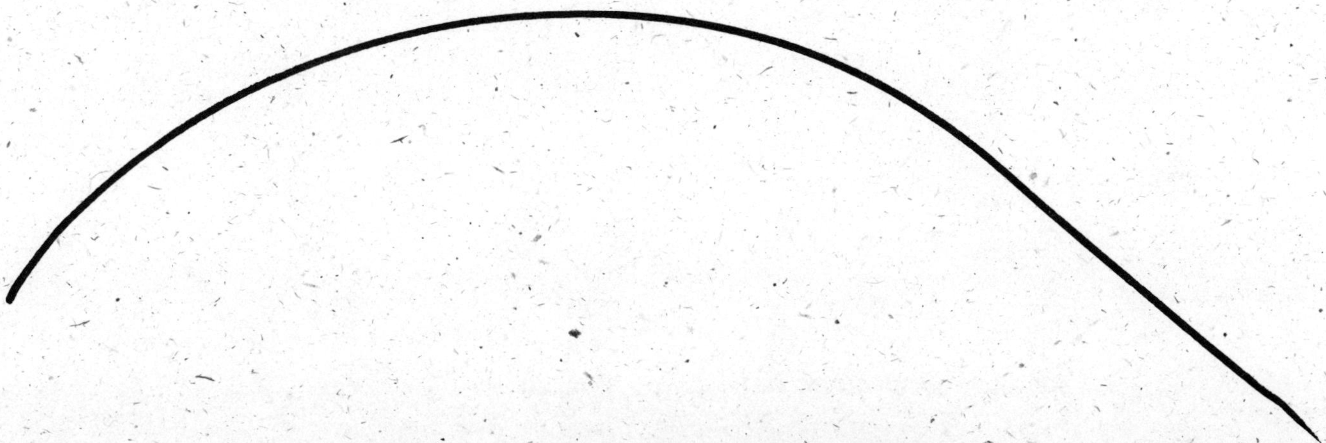

It travels in circuits and byways.

But when we slump or stand up too straight,

it quickly
veers off
these
highways.

When we do what we hate, or sit down too long,

we split into pieces and fragments — "suck in your gut"

"shoulders back"

"use your head"

"hold your tongue" —

and act as stiff as magnets.

Our bodies are smart, if we leave them alone,
so brilliant, in fact, they amaze us.
They have a sweet grace and strength and ease,
they could easily make us famous.

If we keep ourselves whole, mind, body, and soul,

and keep the energy flowing,

it is easy to see, to all children free,

we'll get where we want to be

going!

∞

Later in the afternoon, sitting on a mountain of rock, the traveler looked across the wide valley. She was thinking fondly of people from the train when several teenagers called out and joined her. They jostled each other for seating on the contoured outcropping. Enjoying the view, they talked about the world, and about having a strong voice in the future.

Just then, one of the young women pointed to a magnificent bird soaring above them. They followed her gaze.

The traveler spoke . . .

A bird winging its way in the skies is a mere speck of movement.

But it has a song, a song that pours forth with no urging.

A human making its way on the earth is a mere speck of movement.

But it has a song, a song that pours forth with no urging.

Just as a bird has its own song, so do we.

Just as a bird flies with it, so can we.

Discover what your song is.

It is sung with your voice
with your hands
with your body
your mind
your heart
your eyes . . .

Discover. Then sing out in your own way. Sing freedom.
Sing strength.

Take comfort if your song is different from others.
Every song that comes from the depths of your soul
reaches the ears of those meant to hear. Someone is listening.

The lone bird swooped through bright skies with a farewell dip of its wings.

They watched as it skimmed over the land and out of sight . . .

As a bird dares sing its song to the vast open skies,

so dare we sing our song to the world.

Feel confidence. Feel courage. Feel power.

Sing out. Sing out. Sing out.

Sing for the rest of your life . . .

The melody may change as you love more people.

The range may change as you grow in wisdom.

But it is still your song. It always was.

Sing out.

Only one voice is like yours.

∞

Next day, a young boy led the traveler and her friends along dusty trails into a mystic place of cones and catacombs. Volcanoes had erupted in distant epochs, spewing lava and ash upon the land for hundreds of miles. Rivers then cut gullies in the impressionable terrain, and winds set to work carving bizarre shapes.

They stopped to stare at the lopsided, free-form peaks surrounding them . . .

Sculpted

wishes . . .

sculpted

dreams . . .

Sometimes those who have loved us
and helped us and gained our confidence

expect us to idealize them and
blindly follow their direction.

In our desire to show loyalty, though, we cannot abandon

ourselves.

When we displace

our own needs,

and our own inner

happiness,

when we disown our own feelings, we begin a

slow

march

toward

the erosion

of our souls.

An unearthly, enchanted world awaited discovery. Using hand and toe holds, they hoisted themselves, one by one, up dark shafts. Silently hidden in pinnacles high above the bedrock plain were rooms sculpted from volcanic tuff, long-used, then abandoned centuries ago — living chambers with niches for candles, pigeon roosts with cavernous ceilings, vaulted monastic retreats with awe-inspiring frescoes . . .

In compartments of our minds, we store lofty thoughts of loyalty.

Yet outside influences might have shaped our consciousness

to think that

loyalty means obeying those older, or stronger,
or weaker, or angrier, or more righteous
than we.

Consider, instead, that loyalty means

being faithful to one's soul

first,

faithful to others, as a result,

obeying
the spirit
of love
in our hearts,

sculpting
dreams
of our own.

∞

Outside again, they adjusted to the brightness. Waves of sculpted mounds rolled as far as their eyes could see. There was a surreal look to the scene, as if they were in alien territory. Taking a break from climbing and exploring, they lay on their backs, gazing at the vast blueness above.

One of the older men was stiff from pulling himself up the hand-holds. The traveler knelt beside him and rubbed his shoulders . . .

Bask in the glow of total well-being for it is the natural way to be.

Let energy move inside your body from forehead, to eyes, to nose,
to throat, and downward, until it passes through the soles of your feet.

leaving you

free of

ailment.

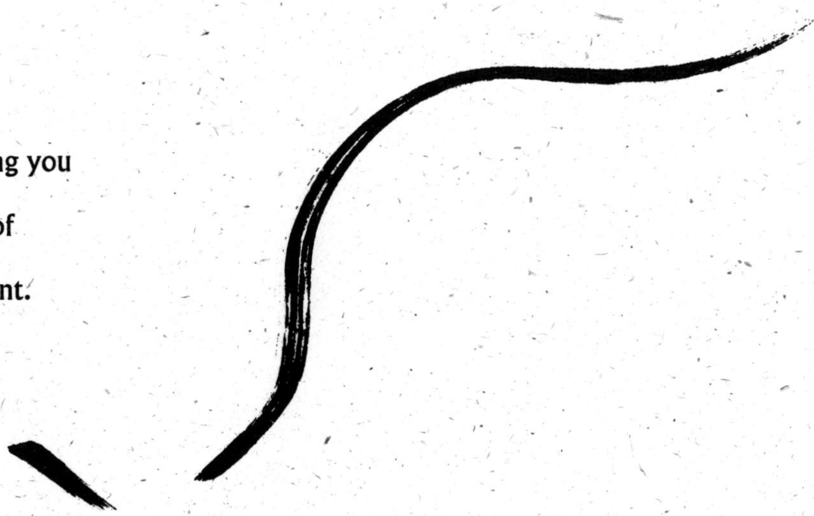

Honor your body in the most tender, nurturing way.

Gently determine what you want and need,

then be an advocate for yourself.

Sands around them suddenly took on a life of their own, gathering in a whirring, whirling dust devil of motion. Stinging particles bit into their exposed arms and legs.

Lowering their heads to the dust, the small group quickly collected their belongings and moved against the force of the wind to a downhill haven. All was quiet there, away from the whirlwind . . .

Do not let discomforts find a resting spot inside you.

Strip yourself of thoughts and worries, hauntings and memories.

Wherever you may be, pretend that someone

who cares about you is stroking you soothingly,

quietly easing

the muscles

of your legs

and body

and arms

and neck

and head.

Surrender to the feeling of relaxation —

peace of mind,

ease of body,

deep comfort of calmness,

the feeling of melting into the earth

and soaring into the universe, at the same time.

Warm your body with
health and well-being.
Welcome radiance
into your life.

∞

Full of exuberance after their rest, two young people broke into a spontaneous dance. Others from the group, and the traveler, began imitating their motions. The girls taught them this song . . .

Hugga bugga whirlygig
Turn around and dance a jig

Take a leg, shake a leg

Give your feet a fling

Snizzle snazzle cuddle coo

Is that the best that you can do

Loosen up, liven up

Let your kneecaps swing

Tiggle tuggle topple clown

Sneak a look from upside

down

Take your head, shake your head

Like it's on a string

Yanna hanna shimmel close

Why not bend and touch your toes

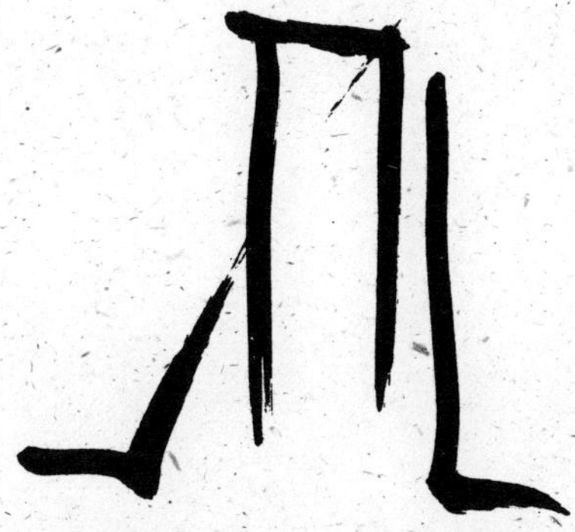

Lean away, leap away

Let your laughter ring

Howda hoda histle hop

Have more fun before you stop

Take an arm, shake an arm

Soar it like a wing

Rubba dubba nugga bright

Now's the time to shine your light

Glide about, slide about

Let your whole self sing

Hugga bugga whirlygig

Hugga bugga whirlygig

Hugga bugga

Hugga bugga

Hugga bugga jig!

∞

Curious newcomers watched from the hillcrests. They threaded their way down rocky slopes when the singing stopped, amazed that the traveler and her friends had danced on and on with no signs of weariness, wanting to know the secret of their energy and joy.

The dancers greeted them warmly and shared in answering . . .

There are magical moments, when wondrous things happen,

when you feel
strong and
loving and
uncomplicated
and joyous,

anything

almost

you can do

seems as if

when it

This is true power. It comes from a spiritual source, with no reward for wealth or fame, victory or blame, only for love and respect, compassion for all.

In such a state of being,

All

things

become

possible.

This is glowing power.

It can light the world.

To order this book for a friend, please send a check for $8.95 plus $1.50 postage and handling (50¢ for each additional book to the same address). Mail to:

Painted Wheel, Box 81406, Albuquerque, NM 87108

Proceeds support the well-being of children throughout the world.